GW00599378

Contents

Contents

HTML

Davinder Singh Minhas

RISING SUN

RISING SUN

an imprint of
New Dawn Press

NEW DAWN PRESS GROUP
New Dawn Press, Inc., 244 South Randall Rd # 90, Elgin, IL 60123
e-mail: sales@newdawnpress.com

New Dawn Press, 2 Tintern Close, Slough, Berkshire, SL1-2TB, UK
e-mail: ndpuk@newdawnpress.com
        sterlingdis@yahoo.co.uk

New Dawn Press (An Imprint of Sterling Publishers (P) Ltd.)
A-59, Okhla Industrial Area, Phase-II, New Delhi-110020
e-mail: sterlingpublishers@touchtelindia.net
        ghai@nde.vsnl.net.in

© 2005, New Dawn Press

Reprint 2006

Printed at Sterling Publishers Pvt. Ltd., New Delhi-110020

1. HTML

Short for **H**yper**T**ext **M**arkup **L**anguage, HTML is a computer language widely used for creating Web pages. Thus, a Web page is also called an HTML document.

HTML is a system for making or tagging a document that indicates its logical structure and gives instructions for its layout on the page for electronic transmission and display. HTML documents have an **.html** or **.htm** extension. For example, index.html.

You can display HTML documents on any type of computer, such as a Macintosh or IBM-compatible computer. You do not have to create separate HTML documents for different types of computers. These documents transfer quickly over the Web.

HTML Tags

Angle brackets < > are used for enclosing each HTML tag and for giving it a specific instruction. Most tags have an opening tag and a closing tag that affect the text between the tags. The closing tag has a forward slash (/). However, some tags have only an opening tag. Uppercase or lowercase letters can also be used for typing tags.

> # <TITLE> Sterling Publications </TITLE>

HTML Attributes

Some tags have attributes that offer options for the tag. For example, the <FONT> tag has a COLOR attribute that allows you change the colour of your text.

> # <FONT COLOR="#0000FF">

Software for Creating a Web Page

There are several types of programs to choose from while creating a Web page.

Text Editor

To create and edit documents that contain only text, a **text editor** can be used. Advanced editing and formatting features are not present in this simple program. Notepad for Windows and Simple Text for Macintosh are well-known text editors.

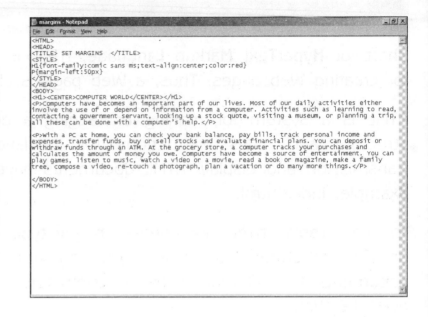

Word Processors

Advanced editing and formatting features are provided by a word processor. Any formatting you apply to text will not appear when you view your documents on the Web, unless the formatting is given in the form of a tag.

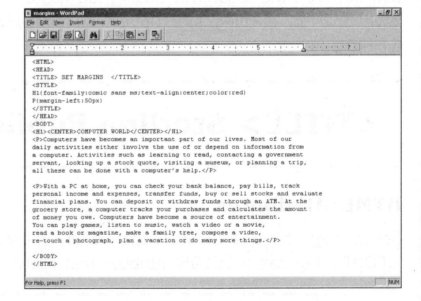

Creating and Saving a Web Page

Open the text editor or word processor that you will use to create a Web page. In the following example, we will work in Microsoft WordPad.

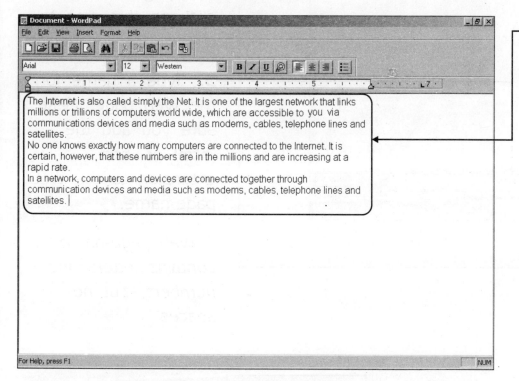

1. Type the text that you want to display on the Web page.

In order to format the text, you must use HTML tags.

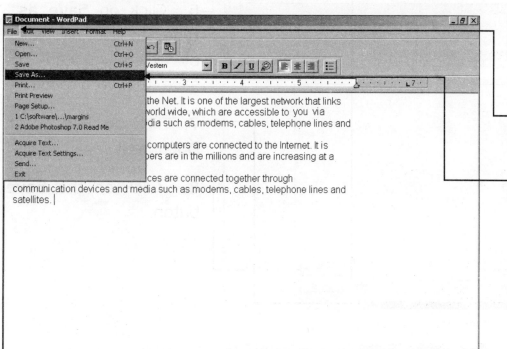

2. Check the Web page for any spelling and grammar errors.

3. Click on **File** on the menu bar.

4. Click on **Save As** to save the Web page.

*The **Save As** dialog box appears.*

This area shows the location where the program will store the Web page. You can click on this area to change the location.

5. Type a name for the Web page. Make sure you add the **.html** or **.htm** extension to the Web page-name.

A Web page-name contains letters and numbers, but no spaces.

6. Click on **Save as type:** to list the ways by which you can save the Web page.

7. Click on Text Document.

8. Click on the **Save** buton.

BASIC TAGS

HTML Tags

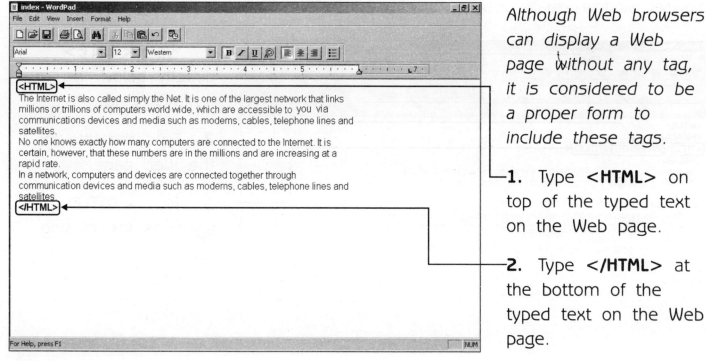

Although Web browsers can display a Web page without any tag, it is considered to be a proper form to include these tags.

1. Type **<HTML>** on top of the typed text on the Web page.

2. Type **</HTML>** at the bottom of the typed text on the Web page.

HEAD Tags

Any information about a Web page, such as the title, is contained in the **HEAD** tag.

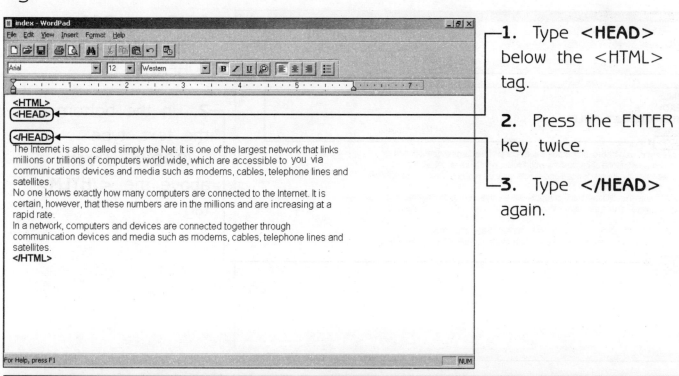

1. Type **<HEAD>** below the <HTML> tag.

2. Press the ENTER key twice.

3. Type **</HEAD>** again.

TITLE Tags

The contents of a Web page is described by the **Title**. The title bar of a Web browser window usually displays the title.

1. Type **<TITLE>** directly below the <HEAD> tag.

2. Type the title for the Web page.

3. Type **</TITLE>** again as the closing tag.

BODY Tags

After entering the Title tag, the next step is to enter the **Body** tag.

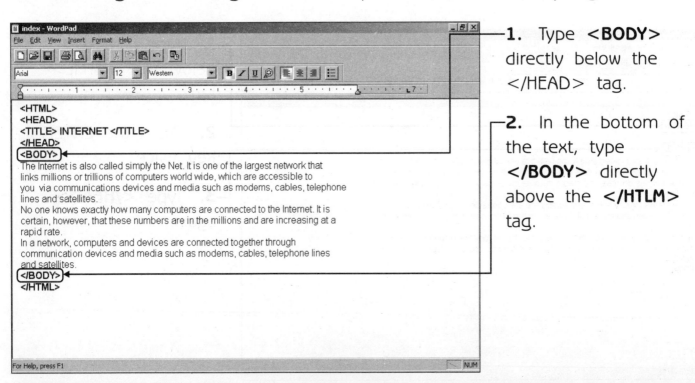

1. Type **<BODY>** directly below the </HEAD> tag.

2. In the bottom of the text, type **</BODY>** directly above the **</HTLM>** tag.

Displaying a Web Page in a Web Browser

You can also display a Web page in a Web browser. This will allow you to see how your Web page will appear on the Web.

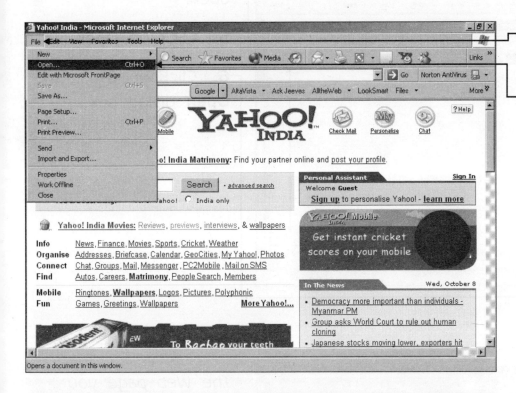

1. Click on **File** on the menu bar.

2. Click on **Open** in the File menu.

*The **Open** dialog box will appear.*

3. Click on **Browse** in the Open dialog box to locate the Web page on your computer.

*The **Microsoft Internet Explorer** dialog box appears.*

4. Click on the Web page you want to open.

5. Click on **Open**.

6. Click on **OK** in the **Open** dialog box.

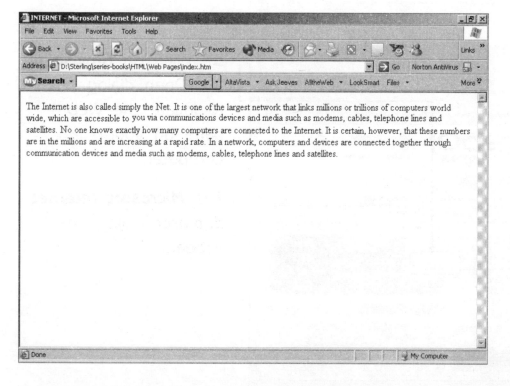

The Web page you selected, appears in the Web browser.

New Paragraph

You must specify where to start a new paragraph while creating a Web page.

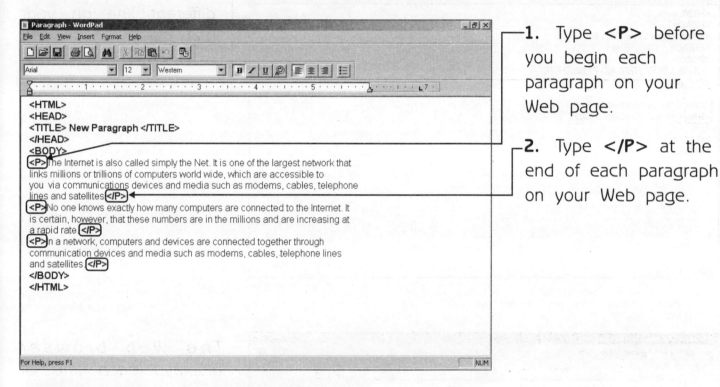

1. Type **<P>** before you begin each paragraph on your Web page.

2. Type **</P>** at the end of each paragraph on your Web page.

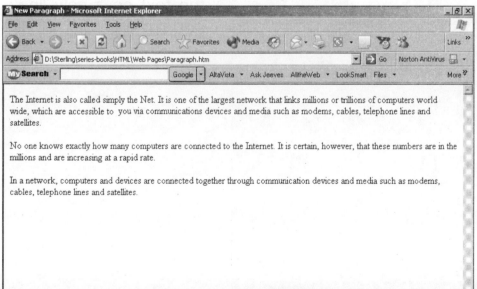

You can see the Web page appear in the Web browser.

New Line

While creating a Web page, you must specify where to start each new line of the text.

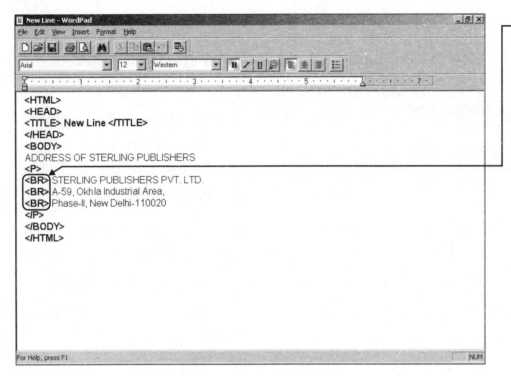

1. Type **
** before each line, which you wish to appear on a different line on your Web page.

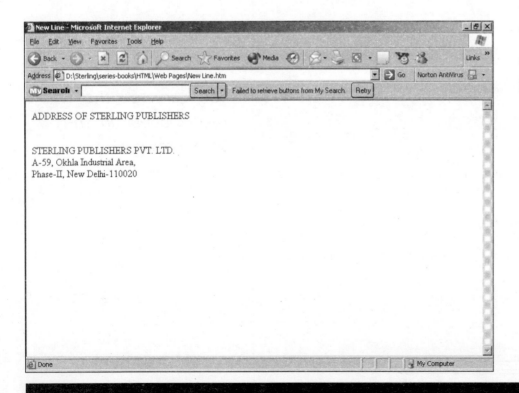

The Web browser displays each line of the text on a new line.

Adding a Heading

You can add headings to display important information on the Web. There are six different heading-levels to choose from.

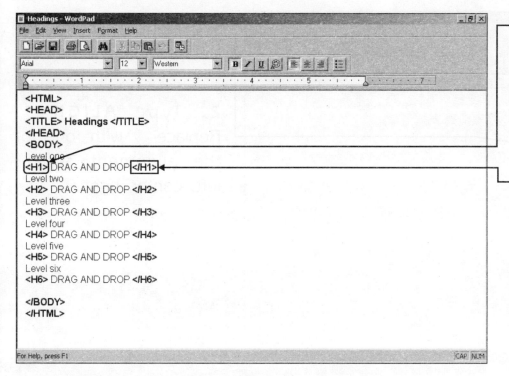

1. Type **<H*>** before the text you want to make a heading. Replace ***** with the heading-level numbered from 1 to 6.

2. Type **</H*>** after the text you want to make a heading. Replace ***** with the heading-level numbered from 1 to 6.

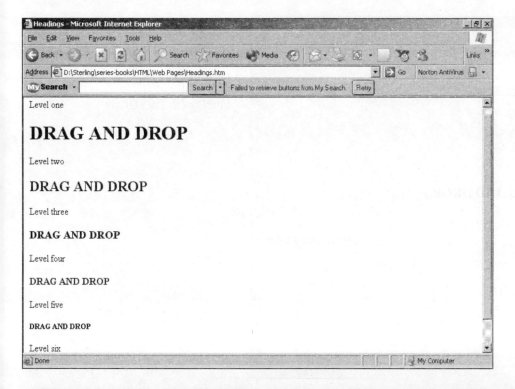

The Web browser displays each line of the text with a different style of heading.

Changing the Alignment of the Heading

You can make the heading right, left or center aligned according to the demand of the Web page.

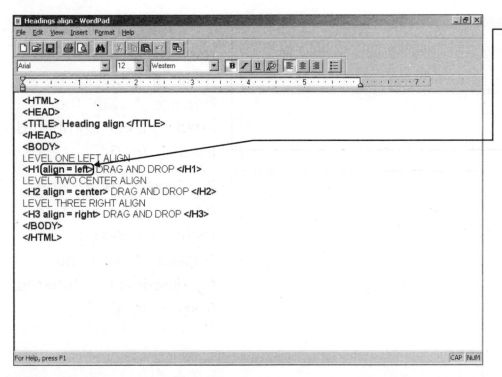

1. Type **<H*>** tag for the heading you want to use.

2. Type **ALIGN=***. Replace ***** with one of the alignment styles: left, center, right

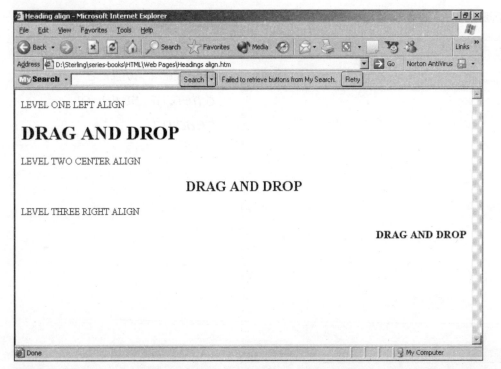

The heading, with the alignment you selected, is displayed by the Web browser.

Center Aligning the Text

By center aligning the text, we can emphasize on some important information.

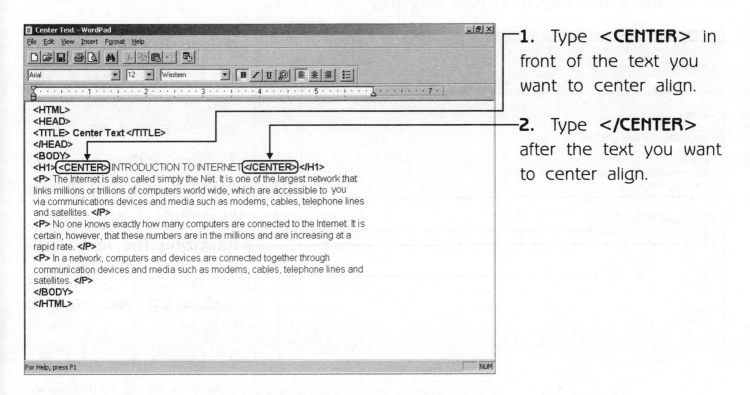

1. Type **<CENTER>** in front of the text you want to center align.

2. Type **</CENTER>** after the text you want to center align.

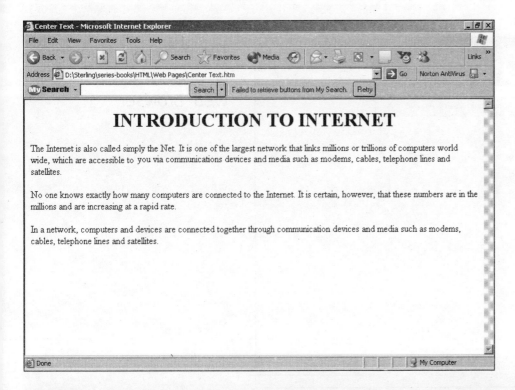

The text gets center aligned on the Web page in your Web browser.

Making Bold or Italicizing the Text

You can change the appearance of the text by making it bold or italic to emphasize an important information on your Web page.

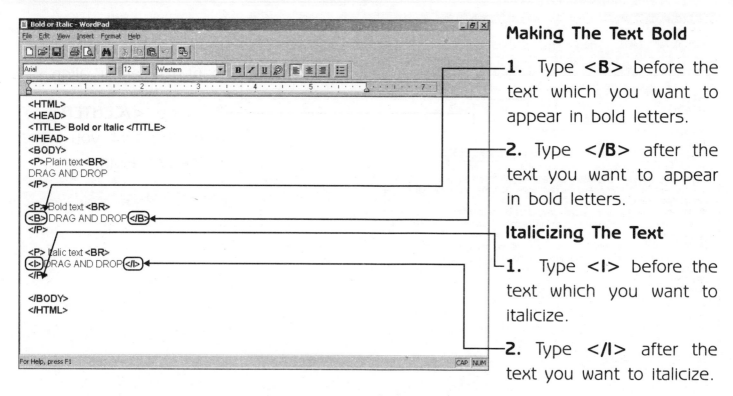

Making The Text Bold

1. Type **<B>** before the text which you want to appear in bold letters.

2. Type **</B>** after the text you want to appear in bold letters.

Italicizing The Text

1. Type **<I>** before the text which you want to italicize.

2. Type **</I>** after the text you want to italicize.

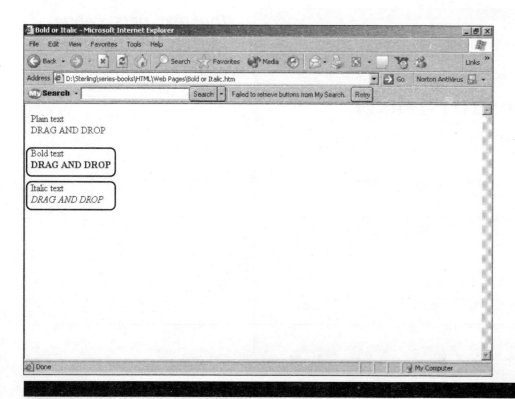

The bold or italic text is displayed by the Web browser.

Underlining or Striking Out the Text

You can underline some important information in the text to highlight it or you can even strike out parts in your text to make changes.

Underlining Text

1. Type **<U>** before the text you want to underline.

2. Type **</U>** after the text you want to underline.

Striking Out Text

1. Type **<STRIKE>** before the text which you want to strike out.

2. Type **</STRIKE>** after the text you want to strike out.

The underlined text or the text you have striked out is displayed by the Web browser.

Changing the Font of the Text

You can change the font of your text in order to enhance its appearance. You should choose from common font styles such as Arial, Times New Roman, etc. This increases the portability of your Web page.

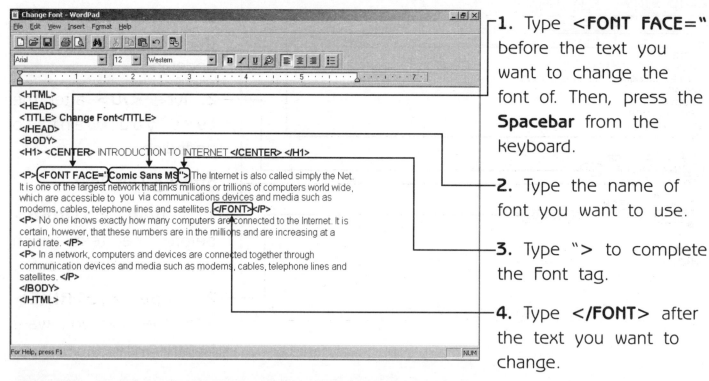

1. Type **<FONT FACE="** before the text you want to change the font of. Then, press the **Spacebar** from the keyboard.

2. Type the name of font you want to use.

3. Type "**>** to complete the Font tag.

4. Type **</FONT>** after the text you want to change.

The text with the changed font gets displayed in your Web browser.

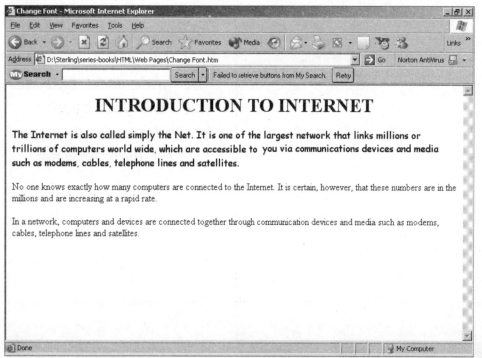

Changing the Font Size

You can even change the size of text on your Web page, just as you can change the font of the text. Along with this you can also change the size of individual characters on your Web page.

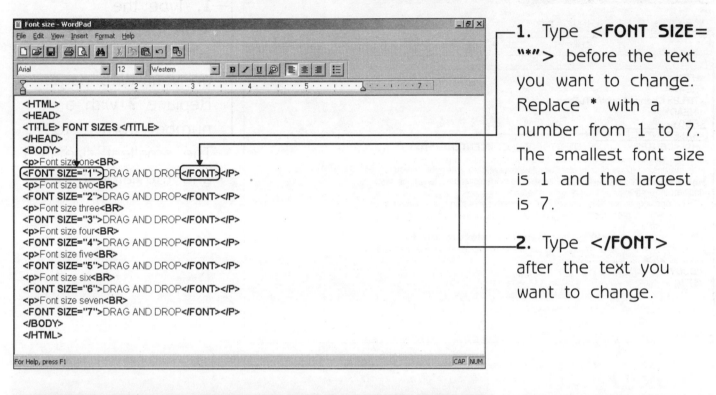

1. Type **<FONT SIZE= "*">** before the text you want to change. Replace ***** with a number from 1 to 7. The smallest font size is 1 and the largest is 7.

2. Type **</FONT>** after the text you want to change.

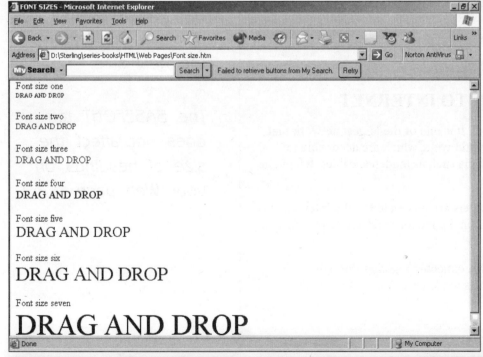

The Web browser displays the selected text in the new size.

Changing the Font Size of the Whole Text

The size of the whole text on your Web page can also be changed.

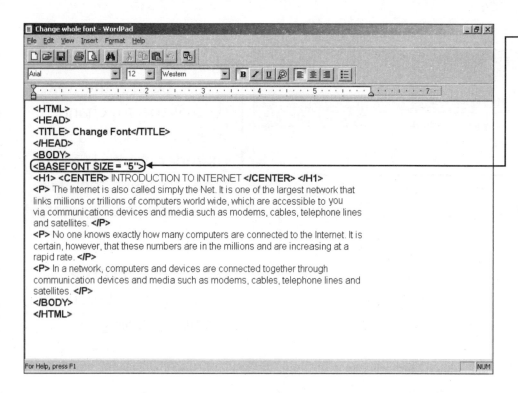

1. Type the **<BASEFONT SIZE ="?">** before the text on your Web page. Replace **?** with a number from 1 to 7. The smallest size is 1 and the largest is 7.

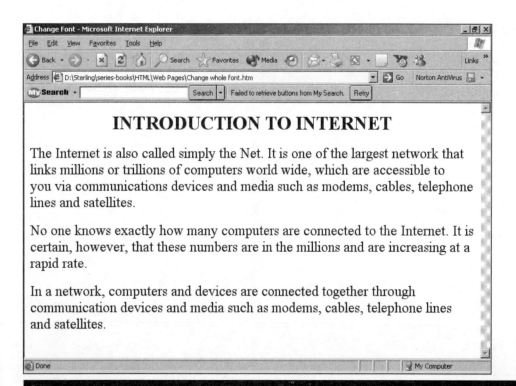

The Web browser displays the text in the new size.

The BASEFONT tag does not affect the size of headings on your Web page.

Changing the Color of Text

You can change the color of the whole text of your Web page. You can create interesting text by changing the color of the text.

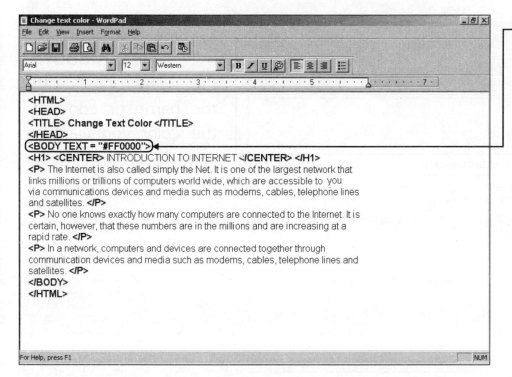

1. Type **TEXT ="*"** in the **<BODY>** tag, replacing * with the name or code of the color you want to use.

For example, if you want to change the text into red color, type: **<BODY TEXT = "FF0000">**

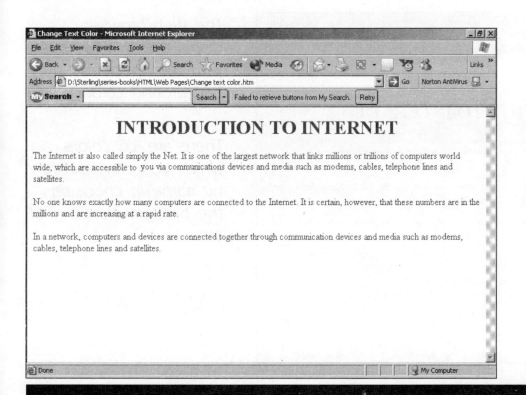

The Web page with the font color you specified is displayed by the Web browser.

There are 16 different colors which you can specify by name in choosing the font color of your text.

Changing the Background Color

By changing the background color, you can make your Web page look more attractive and enhance the appearance of your text.

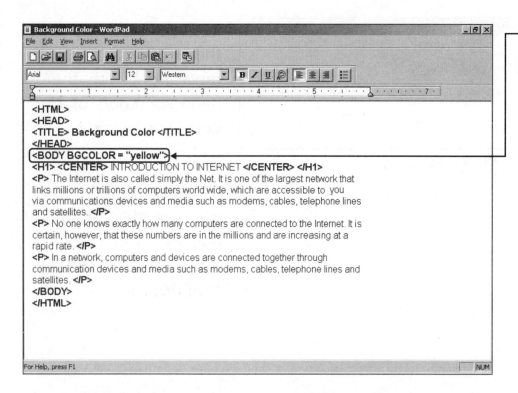

1. Type **BGCOLOR ="*"** in the **<BODY>** tag, replacing * with the name or code of the color you want to use.

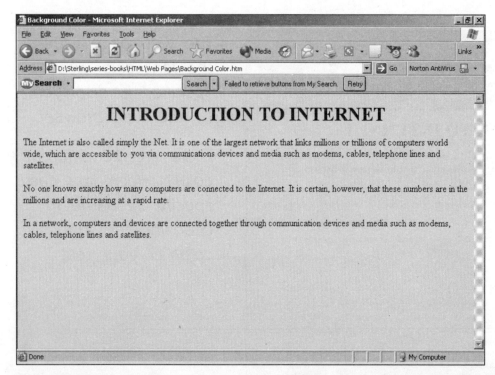

The Web browser displays the Web page with the specified background color.

There are 16 colors which you can specify by name in choosing the background color of your text.

Creating an Ordered List

You can create an ordered list for displaying the items in your text in a specified order. For example, set of instructions or a table of contents. Various styles can be followed in creating a list.

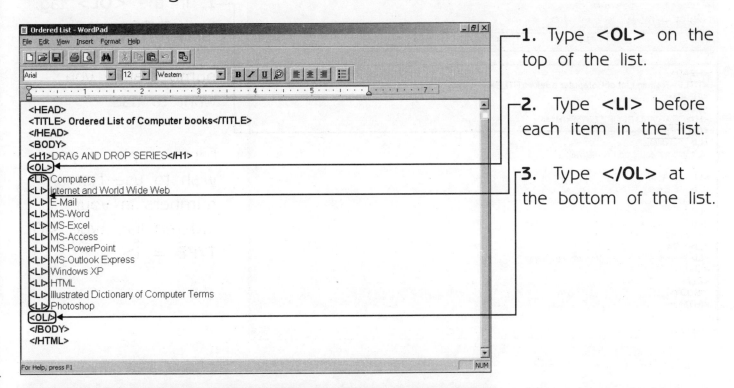

1. Type **<OL>** on the top of the list.

2. Type **<LI>** before each item in the list.

3. Type **</OL>** at the bottom of the list.

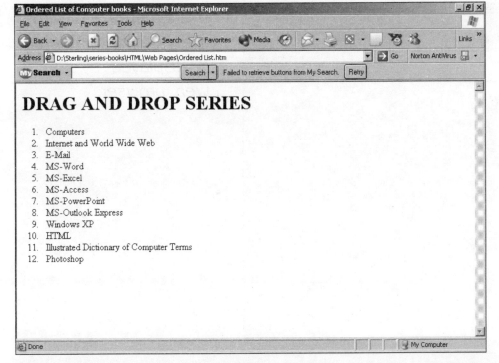

The ordered list is displayed by the Web browser. A number appears before each item in the list.

Changing the style of the List

You can change the style of the number in an ordered list.

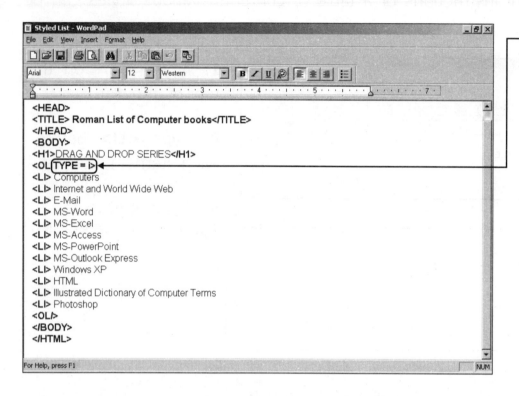

1. In the **<OL>** tag, type **TYPE = *** , replacing ***** with the number style you want to use.

For example, if you wish to use Roman numbers in your ordered list, type **<OL TYPE = i>**.

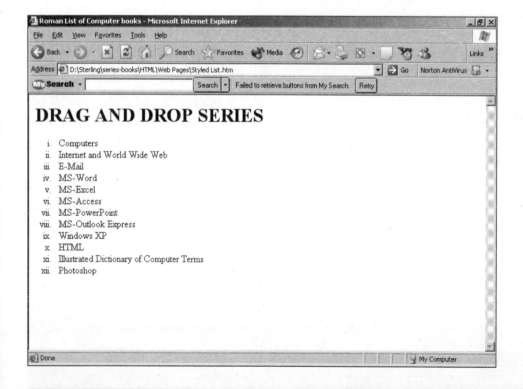

The ordered list with the Roman numbers is displayed by the Web browser.

5. Add Images in Web Page

IMAGES

An image plays a very important role on the Web page. As you have already seen that the Web provides a variety of pictures and images. A Web page can display drawings, paintings or computer-generated art. Companies can display their products on the Web page so that people can view them and make purchase online.

A concept which is difficult to explain in the text can be explained with the help of pictures on the Web page. Readers can select the images to move backward or forward through your Web pages. Most Web sites offer you free images on your Web pages.

You can scan photographs, logos and drawings with the help of a scanner and then use the scanned images on your Web pages. Before using the image, you must make sure that these images are in a format that Web browsers can display, such as **GIF** or **JPEG**. Higher resolution images are sharper and more detailed. Most computer monitors display images at a resolution of 72 dots per inch (dpi), which is considered good enough for use on Web pages. The only drawback is that the viewer cannot get a paper copy of the image. Higher the resolution, the longer it takes to transfer to a computer. The images you add to your Web pages should be less than 620 pixels wide. A wider image may not fit on some computer screens.

If an image you want to add to a Web page is stored in the same folder as the Web page, you can specify just the name of the image (example: internet.jpg) in order to add it to your Web page. If an image is stored in a sub-folder, you must specify the name of the sub-folder and the name of the image (example: images/internet.jpg).

IMG (Image Element)

IMG stands for 'image'. It tells the browser where an image is located on the page. The image will pop up right where you write in the image tag. **SRC** stands for 'source'. This again is an attribute, a command inside a command. It tells the browser where to go to find the image. It's best for you to place the images you want to use in the same directory as the page. This way you can identify for the image by its name.

The IMG tag which specifies an image is displayed in HTML document. The IMG element has SRC, ALIGN, BORDER, HEIGHT, WIDTH and ALT as its attributes.

<IMG SRC="computer.jpg">

Adding an Image

You can add an image to convey the purpose and enhance the looks of your Web page. You should store all of your Web pages and images in one folder in your computer.

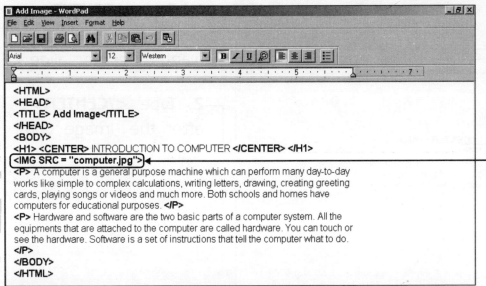

1. Place the cursor where you want to insert the image.

2. Type **<IMG SRC="*">**, replacing ***** with the name of the image file.

The Web browser displays the image on your Web page.

While typing the name of the image file in step 2, make sure that this computer.jpg file exists in the folder in which your Web page is stored. If not, then you have to specify the full path to the location of the file.

Centre Align an Image

To center align an image, perform the following steps:

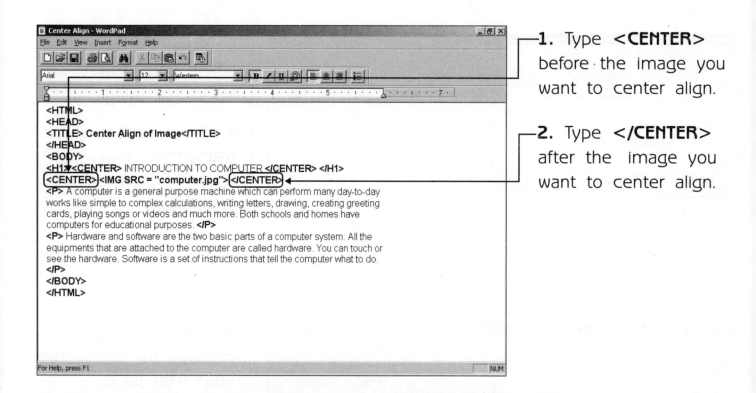

1. Type **<CENTER>** before the image you want to center align.

2. Type **</CENTER>** after the image you want to center align.

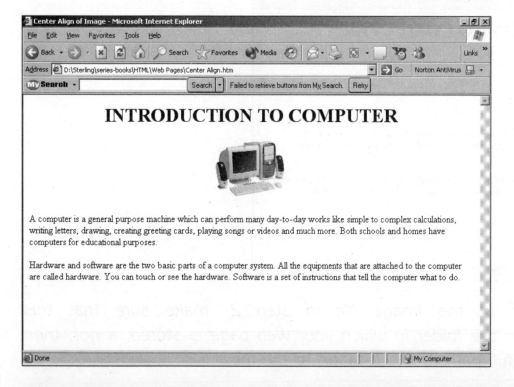

The image is displayed by the Web browser with the specified alignment.

Adding Border to an Image

You can create a frame around an image while specifying the width around the border of the image.

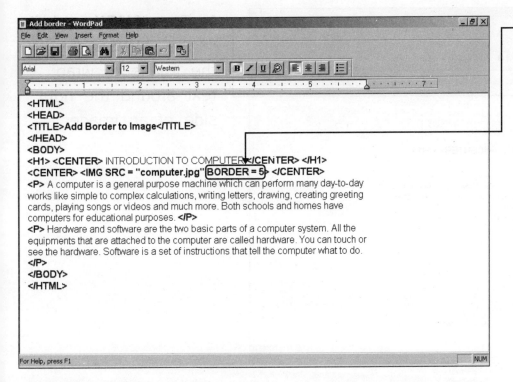

1. Type, **BORDER = *** in the **<IMG>** tag for the image you want to give a border, replacing ***** with the thickness of the border you want to use in pixels like 1, 2, 3 ...

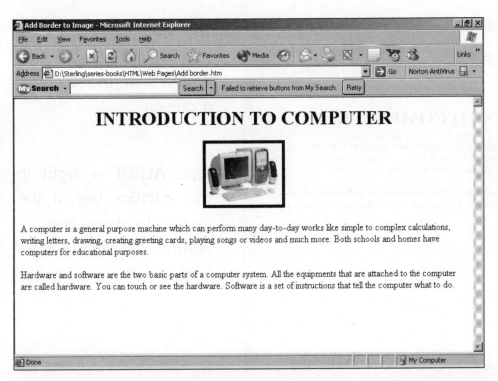

The Web browser displays the image with a border around it on your Web page.

To remove an existing border, specify the width with number 0. For example, **<IMG SRC = "computer.jpg" BORDER = 0>**

31

Wrapping Text around the Image

You can wrap text around an image to render a more professional look to the Web page.

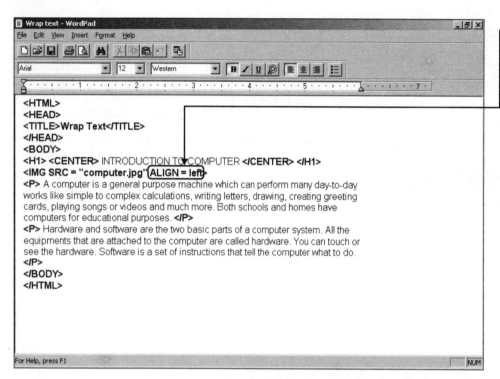

1. Type **ALIGN = left** in the **<IMG>** tag of the image to wrap text around the right side of an image.

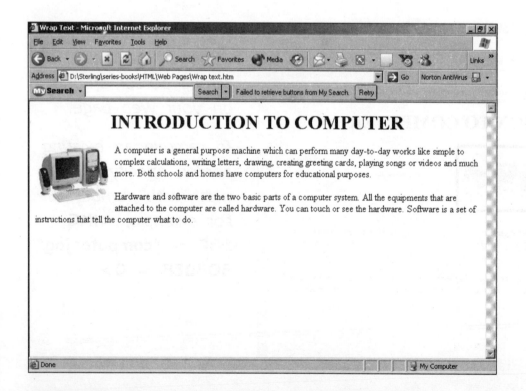

The text wrapped around the image appears in the Web browser.

Type **ALIGN = right** in the **<IMG>** tag of the image to wrap text around the left side of the image.

Wrapping Text between Two Images

You can wrap text between two images to change the layout of your Web page.

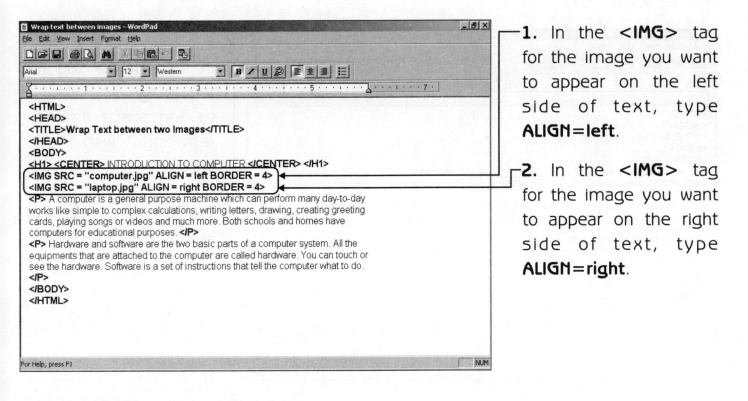

1. In the **<IMG>** tag for the image you want to appear on the left side of text, type **ALIGN=left**.

2. In the **<IMG>** tag for the image you want to appear on the right side of text, type **ALIGN=right**.

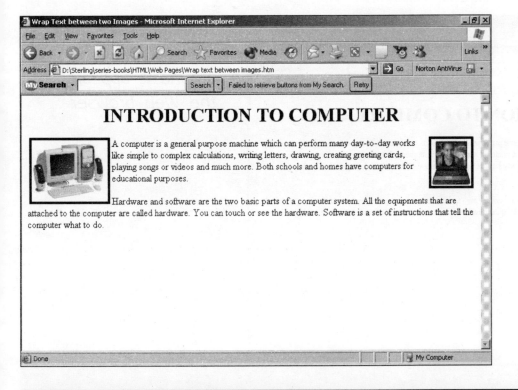

The text wrapped around the two images appears in the Web browser.

Adding Space Around the Image

You can add some gap between an image and the surrounding text. It makes the text easier to read.

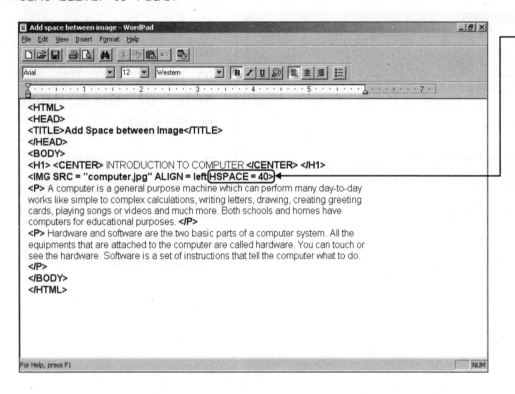

1. Type **HSPACE =*** in the **<IMG>** tag for the image you want to add space around, replacing ***** with the amount of space you want to add to both the left and right sides of the image in pixels.

The image with the specified margin around it appears in the Web browser.

Adding a Background Image

You can add a background image to improve the layout of the entire page. However, adding these background images increases the amount of time for a Web page to appear on screen.

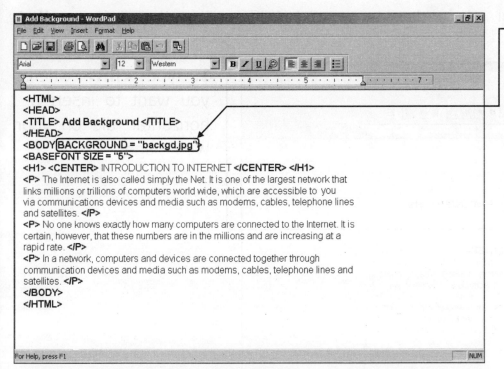

1. Type **BACKGROUND** = **"*"** in the **<BODY>** tag, replacing * with the location and name of the background file on your computer.

The Web page with a background image is displayed by the Web browser.

4. Horizontal Rule

Adding a Horizontal Rule

You can add a horizontal rule or line to separate different sections of your Web page.

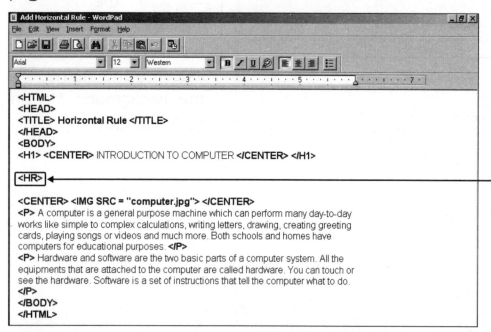

1. Type **<HR>** where you want to insert a horizontal rule on your Web page.

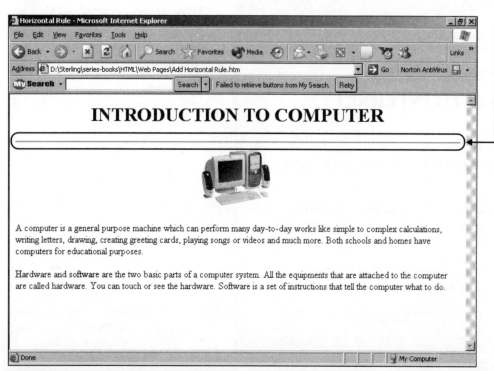

The horizontal rule on your Web page is displayed by the Web browser.

Changing the Thickness of Horizontal Rule

You can change the thickness of horizontal rule in the Web page for better viewing.

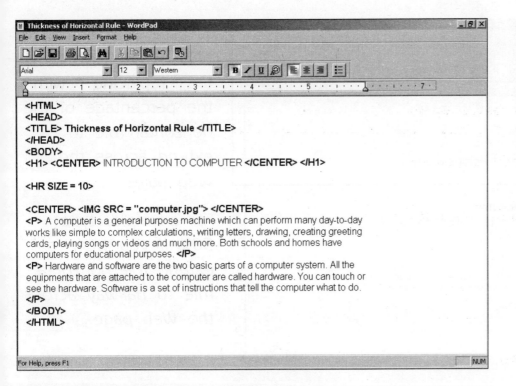

1. Type **SIZE = "*"** in the **<HR>** tag, replacing * with the thickness you want to use for the horizontal rule.

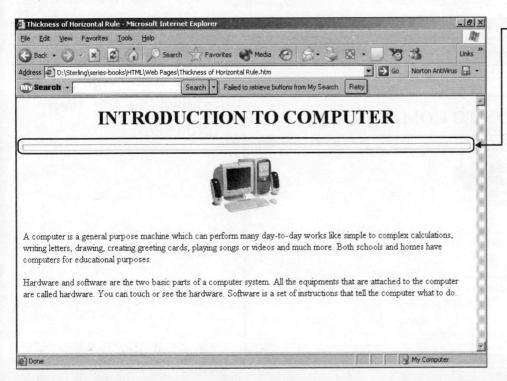

The horizontal rule with the thickness you specified appears in the Web browser.

Changing the Width of Horizontal Rule

You can change the width of a horizontal rule, if you do not want the rule to extend across the entire Web page.

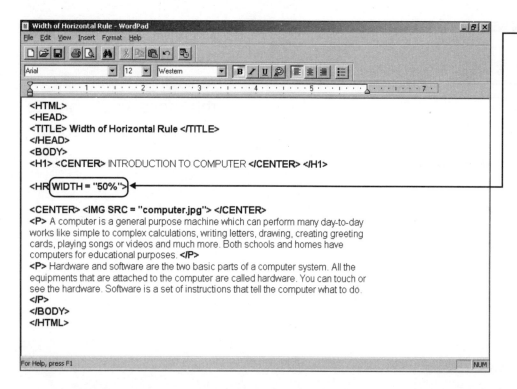

1. Type **WIDTH = "*%"** in the **<HR>** tag, replacing * with the percentage of the horizontal rule to extend across the Web page.

For example, type 50% if you wish to extend the horizontal rule to halfway across the Web page.

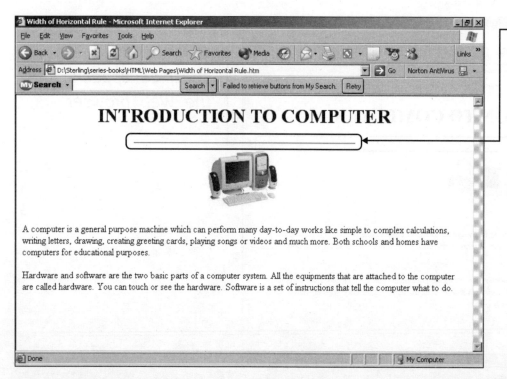

The horizontal rule with the new width on your Web page is shown by the Web browser.

Changing the Color of Horizontal Rule

You can change the color of horizontal rule in your Web page.

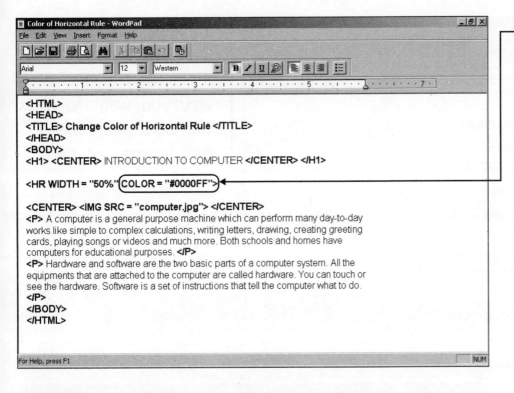

1. Type **COLOR="*"** in the **<HR>** tag, replacing * With the color you want to use in horizontal rule.

For example, type **COLOR = "#0000FF"** *if you want the horizontal rule in blue color.*

The horizontal rule with the color you specified is displayed by the Web browser.

Changing the Alignment of Horizontal Rule

You can also change the alignment of horizontal rule in your Web page.

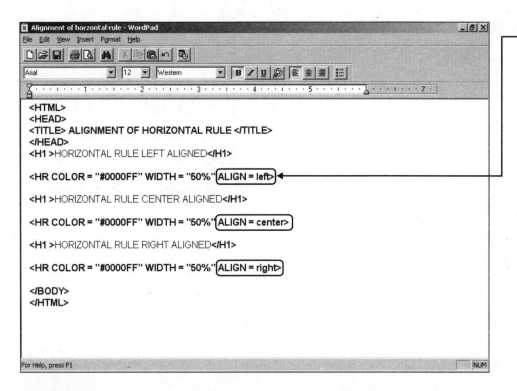

1. Type **ALIGN** = ***** in the **<HR>** tag, replacing ***** with the way you want to align the horizontal rule (left, center or right align).

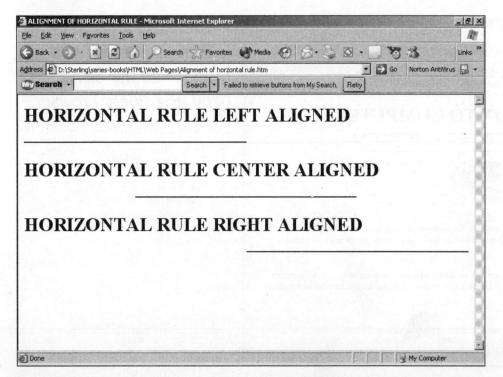

The horizontal rule with the alignment you specified appears in the Web browser.